CARNIVAL

AKRON SERIES IN POETRY

AKRON SERIES IN POETRY

Mary Biddinger, Editor

Jason Bredle, *Carnival*
Emily Rosko, *Prop Rockery*
Alison Pelegrin, *Hurricane Party*
Matthew Guenette, *American Busboy*
Joshua Harmon, *Le Spleen de Poughkeepsie*
David Dodd Lee, *Orphan, Indiana*
Sarah Perrier, *Nothing Fatal*
Oliver de la Paz, *Requiem for the Orchard*
Rachel Dilworth, *The Wild Rose Asylum*
John Minczeski, *A Letter to Serafin*
John Gallaher, *Map of the Folded World*
Heather Derr-Smith, *The Bride Minaret*
William Greenway, *Everywhere at Once*
Brian Brodeur, *Other Latitudes*
Jeff Gundy, *Spoken among the Trees*
Alison Pelegrin, *Big Muddy River of Stars*
Roger Mitchell, *Half/Mask*
Ashley Capps, *Mistaking the Sea for Green Fields*
Beckian Fritz Goldberg, *The Book of Accident*
Clare Rossini, *Lingo*
Vern Rutsala, *How We Spent Our Time*
Kurt Brown, Meg Kearney, Donna Reis, Estha Weiner, eds.,
Blues for Bill: A Tribute to William Matthews
Sharmila Voorakkara, *Fire Wheel*
Dennis Hinrichsen, *Cage of Water*
Lynn Powell, *The Zones of Paradise*

Titles published since 2003.
For a complete listing of titles published in the series, go to www.uakron.edu/uapress/poetry

CARNIVAL

Jason Bredle

The University of Akron Press
Akron, Ohio

16 15 14 13 12 5 4 3 2 1

LIBRARY OF CONGRESS CATALOGING-IN-PUBLICATION DATA
Bredle, Jason.
Carnival / Jason Bredle.
p. cm. — (Akron series in poetry)
ISBN 978-1-937378-17-2 (hardback) — ISBN 978-1-937378-18-9 (paperback)
I. Title.
PS3602.R435C37 2012
811'.6–DC23
2012022917

The paper used in this publication meets the minimum requirements of ANSI/NISO Z39.48–1992 (Permanence of Paper). ∞

Cover: "*The Barnum & Bailey Greatest Show on Earth,*" LC-USZC4-1339, from the Library of Congress. Cover design: Zac Bettendorf

Carnival was designed and typeset by Amy Freels in Stone Print, printed on sixty-pound natural, and bound by BookMasters of Ashland, Ohio.

CONTENTS

I'm at the crest.
—Juphouto Bayasi

for Giancarlo

PROLOGUE

How many crescendos
can someone feel at the same time?

Where does body end
and skin begin?

Why should we pull the butterfly
from the soap?

It's all I do.
All I do is think about it.

I'm afraid my teeth might be controlling my mind,
right now there's a star exploding above us

and we don't even know it
and so forth.

CITY OF LAVENDER

I had everything I ever wanted to say to you organized in my head but forgot it all when you took my palm in your hand and with your index finger wrote "disaster." If you were to ask me how I ended up here, I don't even know. Every night at 8:25 I can't believe it's already 8:25 and I'm so happy it's only 8:25. Sometimes I find tragedy reassuring. Sometimes I want to cry. Sometimes I want to sit in a quiet place. It's within me to rip my own head off. I don't want to think about where I've been or where I'm going. Can't you see what type of person I am? Let me tell you about the city. It's a city of lavender. I can't remember its name. There are a lot of bank holidays.

HOLE IN MY HEART

It looks like I'll be cuddling up in the warm, soft arms of depression again this winter. I'm already hearing the voices. Major in political science. Get a job. Go back for a Master's in political science. Why don't you ask your friends how they imagine their funerals and who they think will attend. Do I look like I'm falling apart? A cookie appears in my hand and I eat it. I'm an idiot with no lips in a city where everyone is whistling. I'm preparing my boat to sail on the high seas of despair. Will this be another declaration of suicide? Reality has become obsolete. There's a reason night has a feminine article. The hole in my heart has gotten so big I can feel it and I can't deal with it anymore.

PEP TALK

It starts with the Santa Ana winds. High-pitched noises begin to irritate you. Are you ready for me to say something controversial? I'm going to make a wolf mate with a puma and there's nothing you can do about it. Things like this usually happen in more sinister provinces. The villagers know something you don't. Should you follow that dwarf? "Wait, wait, you're not putting me in this oubliette, are you? I'm just a lipless guy eating a cookie." Is this how it's supposed to happen? You start a revolution. There's an empire. Your friend disappears. You're shaving all the time. You insist on driving with your head out the window. It begins to mizzle. Even though it's making you crazy, you're totally going to beat this werewolf thing.

PLATYPUS BOY

A mad scientist, crazy guy, world leader, and costumed vigilante have gathered to discuss the fate of the planet. I like the vigilante because he could be anyone and has a really cool outfit. I wouldn't want to have one hole for everything, though. You know what? I don't like the taste of oxygen. It's gross! Do you think it's hard to lactate without a nipple? One solution is to turn all air into water. I always begin by interrogating myself: Where was I on the night of June 12? You go into the woods with a friend and he vanishes. Is there a werewolf inside you? There's loud music somewhere. You feel your heart break the moment you say, "You said it, Mom." Yet some of the greatest superheroes have been monotremes. Ever hear of Platypus Boy?

SPLASH COUNTRY

Some prefer an inner tube and water wings. Others prefer iced tea and nectarines. It's pretty simple: Waterslides are insane when you have a beard, but you go faster without one. Have you ever watched the sun rise over the wave pool? Tell me what you think of our newest attraction. Would you like to make love on a lazy river? How about a violent river? Occasionally, I like to drive with binoculars. If I ever have a son, I'll tell him this: You have many chances to be young. I'm the Director of Leisure. My jai alai and mixed doubles tournaments are legendary. I can teach you how to surf. You'll spend your nights waiting for the next day. You'll spend your days waiting for the night. You, my friend, are going to get wet. Welcome to Splash Country.

I.

I wrote this in the Copenhagen airport.
I was eating lunch.
It was sunny outside.

My plane landed there
because of an emergency.
I don't really know what happened.

Someday I hoped to read this
and remember how important it was to me
when I wrote it.

THE PARTY

Las Vegas, 1999, I wake on a bed of landscaping. Across the pool, I see my boo grinding with another man. I hope nobody's drawn a swear on my face. There are so many vibrant colors. More importantly, music can never be loud enough. It's as if I've never seen my hands before this moment. Ja Rule is on fire. What happened to my shirt? It looks like I spilled a spaghetti dinner and all of today's gelato flavors all over it. Please don't make me go in the sun. Do I have all my organs? I just want to find my shoes and space out for a while. The president defines a party as a social gathering for pleasure or amusement. This party is off the hook.

SUBURBAN LOVE SONG

Suddenly you realize you're in the middle of it and it's heartbreaking. You get a telephone call from yourself in the future telling you to run. All I want to know is if you're mad at me. If I could, I'd tattoo your name on my skeleton. I love to look outside. I love to be outside. I love when you touch the back of my head. I love when you hold me in your arms. I hope summer never ends. It's twilight. I hear children playing. I hear sprinklers, a lawn mower. Airplanes descend over the backyard onto the nearby runway. This is where we live. Hell at its most tranquil. To flee is life. To linger is death. The only thing wrong with this picture is everything. It's the eve of a hostage situation. Will you do one thing for me tonight? Will you put on your favorite dress and sit with me?

THE APPLE

I won a racist prize in a crying contest. This is the kind of thing that makes me want to shout in front of a bakery! What was I supposed to do? I answered the telephone. A woman on the other end was talking, but I couldn't tell if she was talking to me or to someone nearby her because I didn't really understand what she was talking about. My head was swimming in sadness. I needed to buy matching sweaters and scooters for all my friends. Evidently she was a really nosy woman who'd begin harassing me on a regular basis. I was supposed to be having lunch with Mom and instead I was having yellow cake from the icebox. I also had an apple. Now, I grew up in Municipalityburg, attended college in Villageville, and live in Citytown, and I think the apple is here to stay.

THE PYRAMID

Whenever I see a rising drawbridge, I consider jumping it. Everywhere I go I like to pretend I'm being chased. Once I shared a limousine with an interpreter at the Nuremberg Trials. It feels like it's going to thunderstorm. The other day I had that dream where I was near a pyramid in the jungle. I couldn't find you and my teeth were falling out. It was as if I knew people but I didn't know people. I'm a quadruple threat. I open my memory book and bring memories to life. Once upon a time there was a neighbor's cat. One thing led to another and the cat became my hostage. Yet he took me so many places I couldn't have reached by myself. I like to think the pyramid had something to do with this. There have been many great pyramids throughout history. If you were to stack those pyramids on top of one another to create one big pyramid, this pyramid would be at the top of that pyramid.

FAMILY FEUD

Quilting a flower is easy. I used to have imaginary conversations all night long with women I loved. The next morning would be so depressing. It's the typical story. What begins as a fun family outing quickly dovetails into bitter resentment and anger. Who takes onions and Grand Marnier to the beach? I've been making up nicknames for the neighbor's cat. I think he likes it. We happened upon a restaurant that serves the best bowl of goo. They say at the moment of death to carry everyone's suffering. I've seen a man shoot a cat in the head with a revolver. Are we watching a fight scene, an abusive relationship, or a home movie? Richard Dawson sort of creeps me out. They say after death our experience will be choiceless. There's a werewolf inside me and I don't know what I'm going to do. I would have written this sooner but last month I broke all my fingers and thumbs in a wide-receiving accident.

THE CHAMPION

Put me in a room with anything and I'll win. Including chimps. If the room is empty, I'll be more empty. A square of sunlight rises west and sets east of my heart. I have to drink so much Orangina by 11:30. The neighbor's cat likes to nap in the sunlight square. He's the solution to most of my issues. I'm trying to be somebody. Have you heard the new music? You could probably snap my shins in half right now. There are a lot of white towels covered with blood. I'm prepared to hold a revolver to the cat's head, hold the cat to the window and yell, "I'll freaking do it, man!" at any moment. There are a million things I have to tell you. When my heart darkens, I lie in a corner and the cat crawls into my arms. I have to make a choice between good and evil. I'm the most talented raw superstar there is.

MOTORCYCLE AMBULANCE

The road is pumping through my veins, and it's lonely. Ride with me. Some evenings you may settle for the meat of a prairie dog, bat, or rattlesnake; others, you may find yourself in the arms of a cactus. This is the desert. There's no forgiveness. There are only hippies and rednecks. I've partied all night long on the salt flats. Sometimes I feel like fighting somebody in a cabbage patch. Other times I feel like floating down a lazy river in Splash Country. I just want to party without being hassled by the man, you know? Those flowers in her hair are in the spirit of love. The road is wide open, but is your heart? My clothes are always tight and bright. I ride the motorcycle ambulance. It's green and white. It doesn't have a defibrillator.

BATHTUB OF THE HUMBLE ADMINISTRATOR

I have such zany friends. There's the Chinese guy who's always in the bathroom, the guy who won't let you out of the stairwell if you've accidentally locked yourself inside because somebody told you the elevator was broken, the woman who yells at you for trying to organize a Halloween party, and the other Chinese guy who's always in the bathroom. Did you ever find the diner that serves those delicious nighthawks? Here's something I've never told anyone: There are tiny dolphins in my bathtub. Sometimes I feed them tiny fish. After tiny fishermen showed up to catch tiny tuna, the tiny dolphins began to disappear. That was when tiny Greenpeace arrived. The whole thing is weird. You have many different tiny fish in a bathtub, and you have many different tiny people fighting over the fish. And then you have the tiny dolphin, which isn't a tiny fish, but a tiny mammal. What I don't understand is who's in the market for all these tiny tuna.

TINY HURRICANE SEASON

My bathtub's tiny fishing industry has created a tiny community. They call themselves Tinyville. I'm a little disappointed, but I guess it's the best they could do. At least they're not like those dumb fucks in Tubtown. I know it sounds mean, but Tubtowners are a new breed of idiot. Yet they're strong and athletic, which is why the Tubtown Tiny Champs continue to dominate the tiny baseball circuit. They destroyed the Kansas City Tiny Monarchs 13-3 last night. Did you see the game? I like to watch Tubtowners celebrate the success of their team and revel in their stupidity. They're nothing like the citizens of Tinyville. Tinies are hard working, proud, and they've created a striking image of me that they worship, though I have no control over their lives. And that's the thing. That's why I'm so nervous about the upcoming tiny hurricane season.

THE PARANOID AMBERSONS

The Paranoid Ambersons is an interesting concept, but I don't know anything about the family. It could be Father is crouching in the crawl space or it could be he's in his workshop making a rocking horse. What was that rustling? It could be the house settling, or it could be a ghost. What was that? Did you hear that? I hear someone speaking Polish. Wait, that's English. No, it's Polish. For the love of freak, Mother, please walk softly. If I ever become a ghost I'm going to haunt the family living in the house where I was killed. Is it deceptive for a realtor not to tell families about a possible haunting in a home? It's not that difficult to be honest. Everyone on the block knows. I grew up in a haunted house and it's frightening. I'll never play ping-pong again! Shhh! Stop talking so loudly. It's too loud. There's too much noise. It's just so much. I mean it's a lot. It could be Dad's working on his rocking horse, or there could be some type of super scary evil spirit. No, I'm serious. Everyone on the block knows. This is too loud.

THE CONTESTANT

Dunking your screaming head into a tank of scorpions, removing your screaming head from a tank of scorpions, and dunking your screaming head into another tank of scorpions is something you sometimes do for someone you love. Have you ever eaten a termite? Have you ever gathered around a bonfire with gorgeous people on a tropical island and cried as you watched a video of someone you love flirting with someone you hate? Some might say even if you lose you'll still get a year's supply of hygiene products. That's not enough. What does the survey say? I want a million dollars. I want a new living room. I want an electric guitar, and I want Jim J. Bullock, Shadoe Stevens, and Alf to help me win it. Pass me that plate of one thousand hot dogs. If I think of death as a blessing, no one will defeat me. I need immunity from the next elimination. I'm going to win this challenge. That's my final answer.

THE METEOROLOGIST

I like when clouds look like unicorns. I don't like tropical depressions because they're too depressing. What does the index say? How do you feel about scattered showers with periods of sunshine and winds out of the northwest at ten to fifteen miles per hour? I remember when a massive rush of arctic air used to invigorate me. Now I'm lucky if I remember to take a sweater. Often I feel as if a high-pressure system is developing inside me and my chest is about to explode. Have you seen the local Doppler radar? It's the perfect illustration of my most intense fear. I want to live in the troposphere. What do you think of my anemometer? I've never seen anything like this before, but we're in the middle of a tornado inside a hurricane. I have the president calling from Air Force One demanding answers. I'm a meteorologist. I don't know anything about meteors.

THE CLUB

I read something upsetting in a magazine. One summer I ate a spoonful of salt and butter every morning at 10:00. The sports team I supported was suspended on allegations of cheating. My father was miserable but acted as if he wasn't. We'd climb the fence, play tennis, and swim in the country club pool after dark. It turned out he was in an early stage of Alzheimer's but I didn't know it. In retrospect, it was the 90s and the guy was still playing with a wooden racket. There are many clubs you could join. In some you're spanked, and in others you're brainwashed. I'm going to be so late because I have to stop at a bookstore and buy a gigantic coffee table book of old maps. In Spanish they call a club sandwich a "club sandwich." I wrote this, lost it, then rewrote it from the memory of having written it. What do you think so far?

THE BOOK OF EVIL

There's a guy out there who likes to dangle his genitals in his aquarium. I like butterscotch pudding. It's true, I've dibble-dabbled in occult philosophies. Here's a mantra: Go out, go wild, and do it again and again. Out there, conversations about model rocketry dissolve into the night. You talk until you question how you ever got into this conversation about what kind of job you can do with no hands. I have some personal issues I really need to deal with at the moment. When there's music I make up little dances to do with the neighbor's cat. He tolerates them. I think we're in trouble because the cat spends more and more time pacing and looking at me as if waiting for me to do something. I wish I could drink from the fountain of forgetfulness. We're running out of places to hide. We'll have to leave for another place soon and I don't want to go because there's a book of evil buried there.

THE PROMISE

If you're ever passing through the countryside and an old lady with grotesque features stops you and tells you to beware, you're entering a place of pure evil and it's best to turn back now before it's too late; just turn back. Why fight it? If her features are normal, it's your decision. If she has one or two grotesque features but otherwise she's normal, you're thinking too much. I'm really becoming attached to the cat. We're at the lake house. No one will look for us here. We spend most of our time reading, sleeping, and eating sparrows. There's an IGA in town. I set up an account at a nearby video store under a false name. In the morning, the cat gets under the covers with me. We doze to the sound of waves lapping the shore outside the bedroom. Do you like a cool breeze? I've painted a hex on the front door. I think if you hold something hostage long enough it becomes yours. In the middle of the night you ask if there's music. There is no music. Promise me that someday you'll listen to what I'm trying to tell you.

TALES OF THE MOIST

I want to open a booth in the mall called Cover Thy Loins and sell my hand-crafted penis sheaths. Have you ever read *Tales of the Moist*? I wrote it during my six-month stay at the Riverside Clinic for Twenty-Nine-Year-Old Sex Addicts. Would you care to join me for an evening of lovemaking? I don't mean you, but I mean you, you know? Sometimes loving and music go hand in hand. What you're about to read may contain offensive language and mature situations. Reader discretion is advised. "When bodies intertwine it's difficult to tell where one ends and another begins. Everything in the world is art. Words distort who we are. Love is sometimes spoken of as the act of bodies joining together in sensual harmony. My whole life has been a mistake. This is why I'm going to let myself be penetrated by the ocean."

ZION

Here's an important question: What is it, overall, that you're kind of looking for? The neighbor's cat and I are on the run, driving cross-country, each of us with our respective heads out our respective windows. It's typical we don't have time to think about anything we do before or while we do it. Behind every beautiful place is a massacre. I wish I knew what's going on inside his head. One thing to do is cover all the drains, run hot water, and leave. This isn't how I'd imagined it. The sunlight is nice, but I always have a headache. Sometimes we pull onto the side of the road, open the cooler, and eat ice cream. I like to feel the cat's warm body against my cheek. Everywhere you go you wonder what they know. Eventually someone will retrace your steps. Someone will try to understand what you were going through. You're the dawn star. You write a letter to your family. You fold the letter into a baby's shoe. You leave the shoe in a field of wildflowers. I've seen the cat chase and eat a dragonfly. I don't want to live. I wish I were dead. I've said the words so many times they don't mean anything anymore.

GLACIER

I like to, how do you say, watch huge men in tight, absurd clothing elaborately fake wrestle? Everywhere I'm looking at rainbows. How do you say quicksand in whatever language they speak in whatever place this is? Do you find my jackets irritable? What about the number of times I change them? Whenever I pick up hitchhikers they ask what church I attend. I tell them about Pablo going "through the looking glass." I suppose you do whatever it is you have to do to deal with the existential questions. Education is a ray of light! I want to, you know, live inside a sunset with my cat. Do you feel colors? Have you ever put your tongue on a glacier? You can change my sentences. I'll accede to a demand. Please, teach me how I should do it.

COPENHAGEN AIRPORT

There's always the pressure of nailing the first sentence and following it with an effective second sentence. The third sentence is also difficult. By the fourth sentence the reader should have an idea where the writing is going, and the fifth sentence should take the reader there. But what if the fourth sentence is a question? It's fine as long as you end up in the Copenhagen airport. The sixth sentence should talk about itself, and the seventh sentence should punctuate the fifth sentence. I'm in the Copenhagen airport! The eighth sentence should mention the airport, and the ninth sentence should move toward wrapping the whole thing up. It doesn't really matter if it doesn't make sense. This is the tenth sentence. You're in the Copenhagen airport.

II.

I felt sad and walked to the playground.
Everyone who used to be there had gone home.
I played baseball with Hiroshi.

We built a castle in the sandbox.
If only it wasn't empty, Hiroshi said.
I agreed.

I've read Rimbaud's letters.
I used to hate sand.
Now I can't get enough of it.

THE PROSELYTIZER

Emotionally speaking, I'm a mess. Have you ever read what's-his-name? Richard Dawkins sort of creeps me out. Space and time are a fabric that surrounds us. Tell me what you know about the velocity of the universe. What if we're only a projection of an equation? One night, I thought really, really, really hard until an omnipresent male voice spoke to me. He told me I could be immortal. I just had to transcribe everything he said, tell you what he told me, and circumcise myself. It felt like the end of the beginning. It's inspired by a true story. It started with a fist of white light. It exploded. Knife in one language means wound in another. There's no cosmological constant. Look at the night sky. We're someone else's heaven.

BELOVED

She was standing in front of an advertisement for a sandwich that looked really good. She seemed sad. I was at a market across the street. I knew I wanted an orange but what I couldn't decide about was if I should get a pear. I picked most of them up and examined them before returning them to the bin. Did I even want a pear? God, I didn't know. I finally decided to skip the produce all together and walked across the street for a sandwich. By then she was gone. I went inside and ordered pear and brie. I took it to a fountain in a nearby park where a lot of people had gathered to meet friends or eat sandwiches. Then like right when I sat down a well-known raccoon in the area showed up and began bombarding everyone with religious didacticisms. I ate about three quarters of the sandwich and gave the rest to the raccoon.

RENDEZVOUS

I saw her again at a screening of *The Outsiders*. I was in the back row sipping a Chubby and she was with a friend. After that, I began to notice her at the movies a lot: *Red Dawn, Soul Man, Side Out*. What was she, a C. Thomas Howell fanatic? Inspired by *The Hitcher*, I followed her home one night to a farmhouse on the edge of the woods. While positioning myself in the bramblies outside a window, I ran into a highly regarded raccoon in the area. What I gathered from the raccoon was that her garbage paints the portrait of someone who's probably going to Hell. Perhaps that's why she appeared sad the time I saw her outside the deli, I thought. As the raccoon and I settled in for the night, the spring peepers began calling from the darkness. I ate half of a sandwich I'd been keeping in my pocket, gave the other half to the raccoon, and fell asleep.

DRIVING AND SHAVING

When I woke up this morning there was a transient spooning a raccoon in my back yard. Wonderful, I thought. The transient claimed he wasn't a transient but an admirer of my daughter's, but my daughter is fifteen and he appeared to be in his late seventies. He apologized, insisted he was in his mid-thirties and had no idea my daughter was fifteen, then rattled off a bunch of names of C. Thomas Howell movies and went on and on about how the apple is "here to stay" before trying to make me eat a sandwich he pulled from his pocket. The appearance of the sandwich awakened the raccoon, who took half of it and began a merciless sermon about God, purity, and enlightenment. It turned out to be fascinating. I let them carry on with their business. I was going to drive and shave for the first time later and wanted to relax for a while.

THE KILLING

I was at the library picking up Juphouto Bayasi's poems for an upcoming *Chronicle* piece I was working on, and for fun checked to see if they had *Tales of the Moist* or *Panic Force*. They didn't. As I adjourned to a private study room to work on *The Killing*, my memoir about a guy who decides finding and killing his first college roommate would be the perfect crime, I saw you in a corner with a cat inside your backpack. I felt emotional and had to walk outside. The sun was shining but it was raining and I couldn't find a rainbow. My dad once told me about a place in the desert where you can drive your car as fast as you want. I want to learn about it and go there. To be honest, everything everywhere has a hushed undertone. There's a carnival in my skull and it's driving me crazy.

YOU SHOULD HAVE THOUGHT ABOUT WHAT I WAS WILLING TO DO IN ORDER TO GET THE JOB DONE

I found an unlocked car and fell asleep in it. A woman tapped on the window and invited me to her apartment. She wanted me to kiss her arm. I tried to steal a radio and left. I took Giancarlo a puppy and pleaded with him to let me style his wife's hair. He told me to visit a Laundromat. I met a man who put me inside a washing machine and turned it on. He showed me pictures of Las Vegas, and I thought, so this is what life is like in Montenegro. He made me wear my sexual fantasy and walk from one end of the city to the other. Then I drove a red car really fast through the financial district. My best friend had been poisoned, and it was my fault. I wandered the streets so heartbroken that winter. All of the faces looked the same and they were all the face of despair.

BETTER THINGS

I met a man who taught me how to look directly into someone's mind. He intended to kill me afterwards, but I ran away really fast. I went over to Giancarlo's and he gave me a pair of vibrating underpants "just for fun." I taught a class. I attended a gallery opening. I sat in a convertible for hours trying to control my feelings. The big courtroom scene was coming up and I wasn't prepared at all. Love is an animal in a pool of blood, you said to the jury. You should never assume anything. I've since looked directly into your mind. I've watched your fantasy lover untie the twine from your wrists, place his fingers on your neck. I've watched you run from the people who cut you open in the middle of the night. I've watched as you unravel videotape after videotape into the bathtub, saying to yourself, I always thought I'd do better things.

THE GREAT AMERICAN NOVEL

I sat down to write the great American novel. I'd already composed a draft in my head so it was mostly a matter of getting it on paper. I hoped I could remember how it started. I remembered the gist: teenagers on sexual coming-of-age ski trip terrorized by psychopath, etc., but before I typed anything Giancarlo called and invited me to a party. I can't say no to him. When I arrived at the party someone burned a wedding veil, and I was immediately swept up in toplessness. Soon another party arrived, stole everybody's pants, and left. I didn't understand what was happening, but it was a lot of fun. It turns out the entire time I had a piece of corn in my beard. When I returned home I was so thankful to have puke-colored carpeting. I steadied myself with it to keep from falling off the face of the earth. It was time. Phase II of *Operation: Live the Dream* was almost complete.

THE DEATH MARCH

There were six of us. We decided to go to an abandoned ski resort. We stopped at a filling station on the way. We met a European man lurking outside the women's restroom. Trevor confessed his virginity. A police officer told us to go home. We learned the ski resort had been the site of a grisly murder years before. Not long after arriving, a man in a ski mask thrust an icicle into Brian's chest. Carol opened a closet door and skeletons fell all over her. Trevor touched a local girl's boob. We found the European man face down in a hot tub. Susan suggested we take off our clothes and have sex until the killer killed us. Kelly's dying words were, "I never loved you." I didn't care about anything anymore. I illuminated the mountain and ran toward it screaming.

GINGER

It was nice so I walked to the café. A girl smiled at me and I smiled back. She introduced herself: Ginger. I didn't say it but I used to have a cat named Ginger. She was kind of a chatterbox, and I started thinking about how I needed to concentrate on what she was saying so much that I wasn't listening to anything she was saying. She bought me a ginger ale and threw it in my face. I felt pretty gingered out at that point, but as I turned to leave I ran into Giancarlo. It was good to see him. He needed a gun and asked me for help. I'd been down that road before. It's lined with guerillas and takes you to a sugarcane plantation. There's a guy there who teaches the new truth before passing you a microphone and yelling, Joon-pyo, sing! The truth is every dream is a tragedy. Welcome to my tragedy.

A SIP OF INSPIRATION

Giancarlo picked me up in his car with a map to the pet cemetery and a book of evil. I'd been having the dream again. I wake in the middle of the night, dress myself, and lie in the backyard watching the meteor shower until an animal I can't see tears open my throat and I wake, go to the backyard to watch the meteor shower, and an animal I can't see tears open my throat and I wake, go to the backyard to watch the meteor shower, and an animal I can't see tears open my throat. On our way to the pet cemetery we listened to "A Sip of Inspiration" on the radio. A caller was concerned that her husband's penis might be too big. We immediately recognized the voice: Giancarlo's wife. Hey man, what can I say? he smiled and raised his hands. Put your hands back on the wheel, I said. We had so many serious things ahead of us. First we had to choose a theme song. Then we needed to raise Ginger from the dead. Then we were going to carve the face of our God into the sky.

INDIAN OCEAN

I went to Giancarlo's for dinner one evening. He talked about tidal patterns and the Indian Ocean. He asked if I'd ever seen anyone pulled to sea in a rip current. I felt weird. I drank three colas really fast, and he handed me the talking stick. I keep having this dream about water, I said. He showed me his telescope. We watched his neighbors across the valley have sex, and it put us right in the middle of the action. I felt like he was distracting me from something he didn't think I should know. It was time to eat. It wasn't the rainy season, but it had rained so much lately. What does he know that I don't? That's when I jumped from the table and cried out. I'd been listening to the game on my earpiece and something terrible had happened. My life wasn't over yet but I already missed it.

JULY 18

It was awkward because the cat sat on my lap right when I happened to have a boner. I put on my favorite record and imagined winning an important swim meet. Giancarlo stopped by to give me an automatic chew counter. You strap it to your chin, and it counts the number of chews you make while chewing food, he explained. Here, let me show you how it works with this box of raisins. He grabbed a handful and began chewing. Eight chews, I smiled as he swallowed. Impressive. He admitted he'd had a lot of fun learning how many chews it took to chew every meal he'd eaten in the past few months. I can't wait to try it out on some gum, I said. I couldn't tell if I was joking or serious. Obviously I was going through some pretty intense shit at the time. We shared a really little bottle of soda and headed toward Avenida 18 de julio. A person was dead and we had no idea what we were going to do.

THE ALMOND TREE

Giancarlo showed up one day with a "copying oneself leads to sterility" t-shirt. It made my "official t-shirt inspector" t-shirt seem pretty dumb. It was his destiny, he said, to go to his village and kill his father. Would I join him? We drove north through the almond orchards. For lunch we shared mayonnaise sandwiches and milk. We arrived at his father's house that evening and found him already sick with disease. I have to stay and take care of him, Giancarlo said. Sleep here and tomorrow you can go home. I hardly slept, and when I did I dreamt about t-shirts and mayonnaise. When I got home the next day I walked into the kitchen for a glass of water and found an almond tree growing from the sink. I wanted to meet someone who could be my emergency contact information. Tomorrow was a festival day, and I was going to partake in the foods, crafts, and entertainment that had been planned.

MUSTACHE FIRE

I once made love to someone in a portable toilet. I was a knife spreading the butter of life on the toast of the soul. Today no one would think a mustache a mark of the refined, but back then everybody did. Nothing beat a fierce mustache, one that really punctuated your face with superiority, know what I mean? People used to tell me I had a mustache you could really sink your teeth into. One time it caught on fire while I was jogging. Back then I was all, "I love to make love to you," and, "I love that you love to make love to me." I was young, physically fit, and consistently challenged the truth, a dynamite wit who could really solve a mystery. I knew where to get a good breakfast. I was going to win the trophy for best mustache.

ROBERT GOULET

Pablo met me at the airport in a hearse. I was thankful for the ride but wished I didn't have to be a corpse at all the military checkpoints. He kept making jokes about necrophilia. That's funny, man, I kept saying very deliberately. I had two things on my agenda: start a new job and meet Robert Goulet. The new job was amazing. I went door to door, and people yelled at me in fascinating languages I'd never heard. It was the first step toward a long and illustrious career, I thought. After clocking out I met Pablo at the boardwalk to see how many French fries we could fit in our mouths at once. He'd been translating Juphouto Bayasi's work for an upcoming anthology he was editing. I asked him if he thought I was creepy to hang out with. Man, look around us, he said. We could floss our teeth with bikinis if we wanted. It was paradise. He wore what he called wearable art: fluorescent green shorts and a hot pink tank top with a fanny pack and sun visor. I was going to cruise the beach until I met a girl interested in casual, no-strings-attached sex. It was only a matter of time before I learned that Robert Goulet was in Los Angeles.

from "HOME EXILE" BY JUPHOUTO BAYASI TRANSLATED FROM THE ÜL-BEYAZEY BY PABLO ROCKEFELLER

I'm at the crest. I take my last piece of tahil-kin[1] bread from my poköti[2] and bite into it. It's warm. If only I had a cup of bital-tahil[3] to go with this, I think to myself. Beyond the canalways I can even see a herd of omaxi grazing in a field of space flowers. Today I placed my son in a liberation orb and launched him into the sky. My hope is that he finds a world without war. My people have been fighting for too many triple-years, if not with the Pernesians[4] then with each other. I've watched my father and mother, my wife, and most of my friends die. There are three suns here yet I live in perpetual twilight. I'm just an ether farmer. In the distance I hear the mating call of a jacknip. I see the copper trades approaching from the batisiva.[5]

---

1. A corn-like substance indigenous to Beyaz-ül.
2. A small knapsack for holding tahil-kin bread.
3. Common Beyaz-üli drink made of fermented tahil-kin and omaxi urine. Effects on Beyaz-üli include euphoria, hallucinations, fast fingers, increased leaping ability, cotton or wire mouth, and diarrhea.
4. Race of sadists who subjugate.
5. Gauze forest.

from "SKY FIRE" BY JUPHOUTO BAYASI TRANSLATED FROM THE ÜL-BEYAZEY BY PABLO ROCKEFELLER

There's a presence in me—a presence burning like a fire across the sky. Soon the fire will ruin my ether crop. On the cusp of the canyon, I see a family of jacknips[6] foraging for space flowers.[7] After the firestorm, I think, the insects will arrive. I recall my childhood, my dream of becoming a professional spaceball[8] star, how I severed the winning arm in the quarterfinals of the junior galactic spaceball tournament years ago. Afterwards, my spacemates and I celebrated with bital-tahil on the ekali elan[9] until third twilight. I went home full of omaxi blood[10] and spawned with my first love, Jessica. Father disapproved of the ether trade but I wasn't going to peddle space flowers to the Pernesians. This was my choice, and I have to accept it. Now here I sit on the edge of the ekali elan with my last cup of omaxi blood, thinking of Jessica and yearning to spawn again.

---

6. Rabbit-like creatures indigenous to Beyaz-ül.

7. Common wildflowers native to Beyaz-ül. Effects on Pernesians include euphoria, increased appreciation of shapes, telekinesis, X-ray vision, and super fantastic happy mouth.

8. Recreational sport played throughout the universe. To win, players must sever all arms of the opposing team and pass an oobaloo ball through an omaxi carcass. The Phedrons, who transcend arms, have been universal spaceball champions for the past 1,254 years.

9. High plains.

10. When ingested, omaxi blood increases sexual desire among the Beyaz-üli.

STEPFATHER MOHAWK

I was at the scissor store when Pablo called. He asked if I'd heard about Giancarlo. He'd been bitten by a miniature horse. That's a good one, I thought. I asked if he was okay. He was fine, shaken but recovering in the animal bite ward of Holy Resurrection. I'm at the scissor store, I said, but I'll go over there and say hi when I'm done. I was looking for scissors that would give me an insane haircut. I asked the proprietor, Mr. Scissorsby, if he had anything that might work. I do, he said, and please, call me Chad. I thanked Chad, paid for the scissors, and walked to the hospital. Giancarlo was doing well and would be released after a night of observation. I was happy since we'd both agreed to attend a luncheon for people with crazy faces and hair the next day. I planned to give myself a stepfather mohawk. Giancarlo's face and hair were already crazy. On my way out I peeked behind the curtain of a patient who'd been bitten by a zorse and then wished I hadn't.

PLEASANT SURPRISE

I was at the gym toning my body, and you'll never guess who I ran into in the hot tub afterwards: Chad Scissorsby. Chad is a really neat guy. I hadn't noticed in the scissor store but he has a phenomenal body. He asked me how the scissors had worked out, and I told him they'd worked out great but remembered how I'd overslept the next day and missed the luncheon and sat on the couch all afternoon hating myself. I was still new to the neighborhood and didn't know very many people. I spent a lot of time napping. I'd fall asleep and wake in rooms full of screaming half-people then wake again in rooms full of screaming half-people, etc. I have pretty intense napmares. I hoped Chad didn't think the way I'd drifted off in front of him was strange. I was enjoying our time in the hot tub together. Running into him was a pleasant surprise.

FORCE MAJEURE

I was at home modeling a new pair of sunglasses in all my mirrors when Pablo called with news about Giancarlo. He'd been bitten by a miniature horse again. You've got to be kidding me, I thought. Not only is it unoriginal, at this point it's aggravating. Is he provoking the horse to get attention? I walked to Holy Resurrection and found him in the animal bite ward doing fine, though Dr. Wolf-Puma suggested keeping him overnight for observation. I hate this place, he said. It made me uncomfortable, too. I walked to the cafeteria and stood in the corner facing the wall. My arm felt like ice but I didn't want to see a doctor. I couldn't hold anything in my hands. Was this considered an act of God? I wasn't going to acknowledge the life-sized box of macaroni and cheese dancing behind me. I'd be grand marshaling the Inflatable Animal Rodeo soon and I noted everything for my opening proclamations.

ANOTHER SURPRISE

I ran into Dr. Wolf-Puma in the gym's steam room, where I'd been relaxing before a drive and shave I was planning later. I called out his name, smiled, and waved; he motioned me over. He was really sweaty and hairy. I wanted to ask him about the problem I'd been having with my arms and hands, but I didn't. He has an intense gaze, and I don't trust his teeth. He asked about Giancarlo. Oh, you know, he has an ongoing feud with a smartass miniature horse, I said. It's too complicated and boring to explain. We were definitely starting to unwind in the steam. As I drifted off to sleep, I wondered if Wolf-Puma had ever driven and shaved at the same time. Wolf-Puma, I said, right now it feels like I'm talking but I can't hear anything and what's this blood coming out of my mouth?

THE TIGER

I was perched in a tree spying on my own house when Pablo stopped by. It was Giancarlo, he explained. He'd been bitten by a miniature horse again. This is ridiculous, I said as I climbed out of the tree. Giancarlo's shenanigans with this horse had become tasteless. Needless to say, he's been banned from the petting zoo for life, Pablo said. Ouch, I thought. Who was going to pet the baby goats with me? I scheduled a racquetball game with Wolf-Puma to get some answers. This was dumb because I didn't know how to play racquetball and there are laws against discussing a patient's condition with me. Oh, well. Everything I do is to fulfill a fantasy yet realized. In a few hours I was going to rest my head on a tiger and listen to its heartbeat. Then I was going to Chinatown to wear my skin like an awesome Halloween costume.

FALLING FROM A BRIDGE

I woke after a night in the lightning chamber feeling incredible. There was so much to do! It's crunch time, I thought, as I walked to the kitchen for a bowl of cereal. I wanted to grow my eyelashes really long. I was going to sew my arm back on. I wanted to have an adventure. I phoned Giancarlo and invited him over. He walked into the kitchen with blueprints of Holy Resurrection, proposing we set it on fire. I'd prefer to fall from the perfect bridge, I said. We made a list of all the bridges in the city. We chose the bridge on Avenida cruz del sur for its design and historical relevance. As we left, we found a tiny duckling dead in a puddle of water on the sidewalk in front of my house. It looked like a painful death. It made the idea of falling from a bridge seem stupid. What did we expect, anyway? We were somewhere outside Bucharest in the 1970s or 1980s.

I NEED TO GET TO YOUR HOUSE BEFORE THIS AMBULANCE EXPLODES

It began in Jeannine Panda's apartment. There was a hurricane in my pants, and it was raging for Jeannine's panda-like body. It was one of those situations where you politely say you've forgotten to take your eyelash medicine and excuse yourself. I walked outside and saw Giancarlo sprinting toward me with the police not far behind. We ducked into a nearby restaurant, and he told me the story. He'd gotten a job running from the police to enliven the city and entertain pedestrians. Government jobs, I exclaimed. We ate lunch and he asked if I'd like to join him for the rest of the afternoon. Why not, I thought. He really has an exciting job. The police were immediately on us and they didn't let up for hours. There was even a helicopter. By the end of the day I'd become certain of one thing. I never want to wake up to the words you're under arrest for arson. I hope this all makes sense. I'm trying to get to your house before this ambulance explodes.

EPILOGUE

I walked to 7-11 just to say hi.
I saw a group of men
arguing about the definition of modernism.

I fell asleep.
I had a dream about a farm.
The dream frightened me.

I'm trying to enjoy the last few years
before the impending
fall of civilization.

I've learned many lessons, among them,
never put your head into a jaguar's mouth,
even if it's just a statue.

PANIC FORCE: THE TRUE-LIFE ADVENTURES OF REX LAWSON, SPACE COMMANDO

I couldn't believe I was finally in front of an audience reading from *Panic Force*. I'd dreamed of the moment for so long that the moment itself now felt like a dream, though my dreams never had fake plants. Fitting, I thought, since all Earth plants in Rex Lawson's world are made of plastic. "As light from the red and blue suns converged and diverged around them," I began, "an eerie calm fell over Space Base." Five years of pure energy rushed from the page to my eyes and out of my mouth. "Rex turned to his companion droid and asked about family. There are no families, only incubation queues, the droid replied." But there has to be love, right? Please tell me yes, even if it's a lie. As I turned the page and read, "The intergalactic council will never approve of a level five commando passing through the crystal vortex," I thought about how meaningful the words were to me when I wrote them. Just for fun I wore Giancarlo's vibrating underpants. It was the epilogue. This was the experience. I knew it was happening and I loved every minute of it.

SPONTANEOUS OVERFLOW OF EMOTION RECOLLECTED IN THE SEA OF TRANQUILITY

Lately my dreams have been haunted by penises. Never before have I stood on the shores of so many seas and felt so empty. I miss your hair. How are the cherry blossoms? Describe to me the spring rain. I'm sad my cricket died. I've replaced him with a basketball I named Spalding after Spalding Gray. I saw something like this in a movie once and it seemed like a good idea. As you may imagine, Spalding and I have many, many lively discussions on a variety of interesting topics well into the night. Being in one-sixth the gravity of earth is fun. It feels crazy when I ejaculate. I miss your cooking. I want a red cream soda. I want to play catch with a child. When I close my eyes all I see are butterflies. When I close my eyes all I see are strawberries. That shaking my hands do? It's getting worse. If I tell you something, will you swear not to tell anyone? Love is a wet helmet. I can feel it. I'm on the verge of a psychological breakthrough.

CARNIVAL

You forget so much, and it makes me sad. I like holding your hand on the Ferris wheel because it makes you happy. There's one little dude in the Gravitron. A girl with a bloody nose is escorted from the Himalaya. Do you like corndogs? I'm committed to living and dying in the fast lane. I want to lose my wallet on the Hellbender while the operator enjoys a fried chicken dinner with a side of baked beans and coleslaw. I want to win an enormous stuffed pig and save the lives of hundreds of goldfish. Everywhere there are lights and music and children with blue lips. Have you ever wondered what it's like to bury yourself in candy? I'm a little paranoid. If only I knew that in a few months we'll never speak again. Now's the time to celebrate—wear white all week, wear red all weekend. After I die, I want my friends to take my corpse to all my favorite places. I want them to begin at the carnival.

GOING ALL THE WAY

One thing we don't do anymore is go out with friends, buy records, take them home, and listen to them. I miss it. There's nothing lonelier than standing by yourself in a crowd of strangers. My dreams are usually nightmares and never make sense anyway. Remember the time at Splash Country when I vomited in a urinal? I thought there was a werewolf inside me. Man, we used to wear jeans that literally screamed Jesus loves you. I wrote and directed a wordless production of *Who's Afraid of Virginia Woolf* for a silence-only theater. You know what they say: A tree in the suburbs is no different than a tree in the city. Meaning is how you live. Life shouldn't have purpose. We used to take so many photos of ourselves. Everyone thought they were ironic but we were completely sincere.

SYMPHONETTE

Today I was thinking about Pablo and how he'd lost his hearing but for years pretended to understand everything everyone said. I wanted to write him a letter saying I understood but was afraid I didn't. There are always exclamation points as I walk through the city yet there's never any sound. Last night there were a lot of people interested in selling me gold and buying my gold. I tasted an iguana for the first time and ran into Chad Scissorsby. I recounted the time Giancarlo and I raced his car against his speedboat. I've already gathered my knives and I'm going to buy a new knife. I can't wait to see whoever it is I'm going to see next. Until then I have to sit here in silence because any song is going to break my heart. It's bedtime and I need to make sure everything in the house is perpendicular to everything else.

THE PENGUIN CHRONICLES

Six days a week it's a sea of black and white. The seventh day it's white as far as you can see. Have you ever lived where the sun never sets? Have you ever stood on a sheet of ice with a cookie in your hand? I'm all right. Everything's fine. I'm a master of political science. If I learn to hop, squawk, swim, and eat raw fish, the penguins will consider me a friend. I hope they tell me where they go on the seventh day. Maybe they'll invite me to go with them. They say reality is obsolete, yet the sky here is always so blue. I think I'm going to write a book about these penguins. I'll call it *The Penguin Chronicles*.

NOTES

Look for *The Penguin Chronicles* soon at a bookstore near you!

Versions of the preceding first appeared in the following:
Another Chicago Magazine: Pep Talk, Platypus Boy, The Pyramid
Artifice Magazine: I Need to Get to Your House Before This Ambulance Explodes, Robert Goulet, Stepfather Mohawk
Barn Owl Review: Driving and Shaving, Mustache Fire, Tiny Hurricane Season
The Collagist: The Proselytizer
Columbia Poetry Review: The Penguin Chronicles
Dark Sky Magazine: The Great American Novel
Denver Quarterly: Falling from a Bridge, A Sip of Inspiration
Diagram: The Book of Evil, The Club, Carnival, Spontaneous Overflow of Emotion Recollected in the Sea of Tranquility
isReads: I felt sad and walked to the playground, I walked to 7-11 just to say hi
The Laurel Review: The Death March
LIT: July 18, Symphonette
The National Poetry Review: City of Lavender
Requited: Family Feud, Suburban Love Song
Saltgrass: The Champion, The Promise, Zion
Sink Review: Better Things, Panic Force
Tusculum Review: You Should Have Thought About What I Was Willing to Do in Order to Get the Job Done
Wunderkammer: Beloved, Rendezvous

"Home Exile" and "Sky Fire" by Juphouto Bayasi first appeared in *Connecting the Dots: Poetry from the Night Sky*, Pablo Rockefeller, ed.

Portions of this book also appeared in the chapbook *The Book of Evil* (Dream Horse Press, 2011)

Catering provided by Moody's and Eyecon Copenhagen

Punctuation consultant: J@z Palabra

Special thanks: Morning Crew DJs K-Love, Crazy Stuart and the Big Gab, my family

PRAISE FOR *CARNIVAL:*

"It transcends the idea of the book. It's a series of incredible sentences."

—*The Chronicle*

"Is *Carnival* a transcendent series of incredible sentences or merely a series of incredible sentences?"

—*Second Look*

"The world's first real masterpiece."

—*Cat, Dog & Hamster Quarterly*

"Fully realized. One of the best mysteries of all time."

—*The Standard*

"An idyll of restraint. A true work of art."

—*The National Review of Politics & Religion*

"No book beats at the heart of pop culture like this one."

—Ted Wolf-Puma, M.D., Author, *MABU: The Most Advanced Body in the Universe*

"A tale familiar to any teenager, about those moments when you choose what your life will mean."

—Pablo Rockefeller, Editor, *Connecting the Dots*